A Father's Guide
to Raising Boys

....

Rob Green

New
Growth
Press

WWW.NEWGROWTHPRESS.COM

New Growth Press, Greensboro, NC 27404
www.newgrowthpress.com
Copyright © 2015 by Rob Green

Cover Design: Faceout Books, faceoutstudio.com
Typesetting: Lisa Parnell, lparnell.com

ISBN: 978-1-942572-18-3 (Print)
ISBN: 978-1-942572-19-0 (eBook)

Library of Congress Cataloging-in-Publication Data
Green, Rob (Robert Eric)
  A father's guide to raising boys / Rob Green.
    pages cm
  ISBN 978-1-942572-18-3 (print) —
  ISBN 978-1-942572-19-0 (ebook)
1. Fatherhood—Religious aspects—Christianity. 2. Fathers and
sons—Religious aspects—Christianity. 3. Parenting—Religious
aspects—Christianity. 4. Child rearing—Religious aspects—
Christianity. I. Title.
  BV4529.17.G73 2015
  248.8'421—dc23

                                                      2015001454

Printed in China

23 22 21 20 19 18 17 16   2 3 4 5 6

Fatherhood is awesome. Raising boys is a privilege and a joy.[1]

Perhaps, like me, before your first son was out of diapers you imagined the day when he would be signing a letter of intent to play college football at your alma mater. Or maybe you imagine something even better—your son making a difference in the world. And, also if you are like me, in the meantime, you have a blast pillow fighting, wrestling, having boys' nights, and generally going a bit crazy from time to time—just hanging out with the guys.

But raising boys is also worrisome. We wonder how our boys will turn out and exactly what we should do to make sure they learn to love God and others. This minibook won't give you "the answer." There is no fail-safe way to ensure that your son will live every day of his life for Jesus. That has far more to with the Lord and his work in your son than it has to do with what you do or don't do. As a father I am wary of those who act as if perfect parenting (which doesn't exist) will result in awesome children. I make no such claims. To be honest, I struggle with every aspect of what I'm recommending in this minibook. Instead, this minibook represents who I want to be by God's grace, rather than who I am right now.

As I think about parenting my boys, I start with two basic, biblical truths: First, as fathers we are completely dependent on the work of God to draw our boys to Christ (Ephesians 2:8–10). We are not able to make our children believe. We cannot save our children from their sin. We *can* be an important part of their life, but we can never be their hero because only Jesus can be that. Nor, much to our chagrin, are we able to make all other decisions for our children. God has designed each of them to be an individual, and unlike Star Trek's Borg, they are not assimilated!

Second, as fathers, regardless of how our boys ultimately live, we want to live thankful and pleasing lives to Jesus (2 Corinthians 5:9–10; 1 Peter 2:9–10). Thus, whether our sons believe and live for Christ or not, we want to be obedient to the Lord in our parenting. We find our joy first in the Lord and in honoring him. All other joys, including the joys of raising boys, are an added bonus from the Father who gives good gifts. With these two truths in mind, it is my prayer that this minibook will encourage you to strengthen your relationship with Jesus, help you live according to his Word, and give you practical advice on raising your boys in the teaching and admonition of the Lord.

Here are three basic biblical principles to guide us in being faithful fathers to our sons.

Love Completely

The Lord reminds us regularly of the importance of love. Loving God and others is in some sense a summary of the entire Old Testament (Matthew 22:37–40). The New Testament picks up where the Old Testament leaves off. Christians are not only to love, but they are to love as Jesus loved (John 13, 1 John 2). This provides a helpful way to organize what it means to love our boys well.

Love the Lord.

Matthew 22:37–38 teaches that we must love God above all else. That's the way our heavenly Father has designed us. If we love something else more than God, including our boys, we function differently than God intended. The Lord, in his great wisdom, designed us in such a way that when we love him first, the best possible love will flow out of us to our boys.

You probably know firsthand just how difficult it is to love, give, and serve—especially after a long day (or week!) of work. When I walk in the door, my desire is to eat dinner, relax, and be free from the burden of serving anyone. Only as I know how much I am loved by Jesus and that my identity is in him, will I depend on him for the power to turn from my own comfort and instead love and serve my family.

The more we locate our identity in Christ—instead of ourselves as husbands, fathers, and workers—the more we live out of the truths Paul shares in Romans 8:31–39: God is for us; there is no condemnation in Christ Jesus; and nothing can separate us from the love of God because of what Jesus has done for us. Because God's love for us in Christ can never be threatened, that allows us to love others, give to others, and serve others. Without the love of God in our hearts, we will demand love from others. As a father, one of the greatest gifts you can give your boys is a wholehearted love for God. It not only serves as an example to them, but it will also result in love for them that is real, meaningful, and faithful no matter what happens—just like God's love for you.

Matthew 22 does not end with loving God, but adds the command to love our neighbor. Jesus adds to that thought by saying "just as I have loved you, you also are to love one another" (John 13:34). Loving others as Jesus loves us involves self-sacrifice that often conflicts with our schedule, time, and desire to do our own thing. This sacrificial love for others begins inside the walls of our own homes.

Love their mother.

Loving your wife is not only consistent with the call for husbands to love their wives as Christ loved the church and gave himself for her (Ephesians 5:25–26), it is also consistent with what it means to be a biblical father. When you love your son's mother, you love someone he loves. It gives him safety and security. If you treat his mother as an enemy, then it forces him to take sides. It's not likely that your son is mature enough to determine how he can love you and his mother if you don't love her. That is like asking your son to do a triple integral when he has not completed Algebra I.

When you love his mother, you lay the groundwork for a home where parents solve problems, encourage one another, pray for one another, and treat one another with kindness. This allows your son to live in a home where safety and security abound. He is safe to be what God has called him to be without feeling like he has to choose between his mom and his dad.

Additionally, your boys will be in many places that are far from safe, secure, or stable. Friends come and go faster than tater tots on Friday. Ten seconds can make the difference between whether your son is the hero of a game or the reason for the loss. Relationships with girls can foster roller-coaster emotions. Although the world may be full of chaos and uncertainty, what a gift to your son for him to know that inside the walls of his home are love, joy, peace, patience, kindness, and self-control—those essential elements of a safe, secure, and stable home.

It is important for the boys to know that you and your wife are the primary relationship in the home. God says that a man and a woman cleave together and form one flesh (Genesis 2:24) and this bond should be broken only by death (Matthew 19:6). That makes your marriage a higher priority than your parenting because your marriage lasts even after your children grow up and leave. As your boys reach the teen years, they may even need to be told rather plainly that if they force you to choose between pleasing their mom or pleasing them, you will choose their mother every time. It can be difficult sometimes to make this choice, particularly if your marriage is not a happy one or if your wife consistently seems to choose your children over you. But while her choices may make yours more difficult, it is still your responsibility to love her as Christ loves the church. He will faithfully provide whatever resources you need to do this (2 Peter 1:3–4).

Even if you are no longer married to your boys' mother, the importance of loving her as a neighbor remains. Imagine what a contrast that will be against the pettiness that is often a normal part of a broken relationship. This may be incredibly painful and difficult, depending on the circumstances of the breakup, but again, keep in mind that Jesus calls us to love even our enemies and gives us both his example and his power to do so. Ask your heavenly Father to give you his persevering love for your son's mom. Instead of asking your son to take sides in whatever disagreements you might have, you can model an attitude of respect and honor.

Attend events that are important to them.

Many fathers have preconceived ideas about what their sons will do or be. I certainly did. It is easy to place our expectations on our sons. But God is creative. He gives people a variety of skills, abilities, and gifts. Some boys love to do things their fathers aren't very interested in. For example, I don't really like anything to do with the arts. As a child I was bored every time I had to attend a play, a performance, or a musical concert. Even worse was touring an art gallery. In my mind, going to look at art ranked only slightly higher than going to the dentist.

I wanted my boys in sports—any sport, all sports—because I enjoyed sports. But as fathers we need to celebrate the way God has gifted and equipped each of our sons. So if our son is an awesome artist, we tour art galleries. If he loves music, we go to concerts. If our sons love sports, then we find time to be at our boys' athletic events.

Work can wait. The company will not shut down if you attend an event with your boy. Ministry professionals, your appointment can wait. The God of the universe will not be in crisis mode if you postpone a meeting so that you can be with your son. Your boys want you to be at their events. They want you to be excited about the things that excite them. They want to celebrate accomplishments with your presence (and maybe some ice cream). After all, who likes to celebrate an accomplishment alone?

Sadly, many fathers are too distracted to be there. So their boys have to find surrogate fathers (i.e., the fathers of boys who are there) to hang out with. I don't mind serving as a boy's surrogate father at an event, but I wish his father was there instead. Especially in the evenings, activities for my children take priority.

Be affectionate with them.

Another way to show love for your boys is to be affectionate with them. Some fathers treat their boys as if affection will somehow warp their boys and rob them of their masculinity. Yet, to my knowledge, none of our counselors (serving for thirty-five years) has ever encountered a man confessing that his life has been difficult because his father gave him a hug after a game or a kiss before bed.[2]

Boys need your affection. They need to know that they are "all good" with dad. If you're not used to it, expressing love and affection may feel uncomfortable at first, but stick with it. After all, it is an important reflection of the desire to know that we are "all good" with our heavenly Father. Showing affection to your son helps connect him to God's love for him.

Being affectionate in a godly way with your son will also help him understand how to be affectionate with others. How he will relate to his wife, his children, or more immediately, his friends and the girls around him, will be influenced by how you handle your affection with him. If you are uncertain how to do this, begin by asking God to show you where your affection is lacking. Then search his Word for demonstrations of love to his children. Observe the men around you and identify those whose relationships with their sons you want to emulate. Consider cultivating a friendship with those men and seeking their advice. Again, this may feel uncomfortable at first, but it is difficult to make important changes without help, especially if your own role models are less than helpful.

Give them instruction and discipline.

It is easy to get into "anger mode." You know, the mode where you are irritated about everything related to your boys. Their room is a dump; their efforts in school are marginal at best; they walk away from the table after dinner like the maid is going to clean up; and on and on it goes. Let me encourage you to move from "anger mode"—stewing about it or barking out criticisms—to giving instruction and potentially discipline.

Our instruction and discipline is not in anger. Instead, both instruction and discipline flow out of a desire to nurture and mature your sons. You want to help them understand that selfishness is neither pleasing to the Lord nor the proper way to prepare for life. After all, your boys will learn (if they have not learned already) that the world does not revolve around them. This may mean different kinds of teaching and consequences. Regardless of how you instruct and what methods you choose to discipline, the goal is not to provoke our children to anger, but to raise them in maturity (Ephesians 6:4). We want our sons to see the importance of living under authority, the importance of doing their best, and the importance of serving.

Fathers, Jesus said that the greatest commandment was to love the Lord with all your heart, mind, and strength and then to love your neighbor as yourself. Your boys are very near neighbors and they desperately need your love.

Lead Them to Jesus

There is no doubt that it is important to love your boys, but Jesus loves them more than you do. Jesus is the one who died for them (Romans 5:8), the one who is able to give them new life (Ephesians 2:4), and the only one who can forgive them of their sins (Mark 2:1–12). Your boys desperately need to repent of their sin and trust in the death and resurrection of Jesus. Your boys need to learn and live out of the gospel. Yes, loving them is crucial, but more than a loving dad, they need a Savior—and there is only one who can fill that role.

Not only do your boys need salvation in Jesus, they need to know the comfort, protection, and care that Jesus provides each day of their lives. While this has implications in many ways, here are two:

Helps them avoid despair.

As a boy, I experienced a lot of problems my dad could not fix. I went to several schools that were a bit rough. Unlike other members of my family, I was not gifted with many strength genes. I was smaller and weaker than most people my age until I was a junior in high school. So, I suffered a fair bit.

As a father, I am painfully aware that there are some issues that occur in my boys' lives that I cannot fix. So how do they handle them? The answer comes in understanding a biblical worldview. My boys need to learn how to handle difficulties without going into despair. Psalm 13 is a powerful psalm to teach dependence on the Lord. David confesses his struggle with feeling that God has left him (vv. 1–2) and yet, he still prays to the Lord and asks for help

(vv. 3–4). Our boys need that lesson. They need to know that those moments when they are most discouraged are the times they need to depend most fervently on the Lord. Psalm 13 ends with David confessing the goodness of God. Our boys will do the same when God meets with them and comforts them in their toughest moments.

Encourages them to develop identity in the right place.

A second important reason your boys need to focus on their relationship with Christ is because in Christ your boys have a new identity. The home can be, and should be, a stable place. But we all know that stability can be disrupted in many ways. Thus, neither you nor anything on earth can be the stabilizing force in your boy's life. All earthly things are subject to decay and destruction. But when our boys are grounded on the rock of Jesus, then they find their identity in him and are prepared to handle the various pressures they will experience (especially the teenage pressures that often encourage boys to do unwise things).

I have argued that raising boys is about loving them and leading them to the one who loves them more than you. These are the foundations of godly fatherhood, but other important things to consider in raising your sons include the following:

Encourage Them to Develop
the Character of a Godly Man

It would be impossible to cover this subject com-pletely here, but let me suggest three ways to develop the character of a godly man in your boys.

Teach them when to be the lion and when to be the lamb.

On one hand, we want our boys to be strong and able to serve as a protector if needed. On the other hand, we do not want our boys to turn into brawlers, abusers, or simply mean dudes (1 Timothy 3:1–7). Thus, we want to instill in them aspects of a lion and aspects of a lamb, as well as the wisdom to know when each is required.

Knowing how and when to utilize their strength is an important lesson for any boy. My boys are both on the wrestling team, and we often say, "lion on the mat, and a lamb off it." The whole concept is that when you step into the circle, you are stepping into the time and place where the lion is required. Later in life that skill may be needed when someone is being attacked, an intruder enters the home, or military service is required.

However, once outside the circle, the boy is to be a lamb. The time for exerting physical strength against another has given way to a time for relation-ship-building, encouragement, and kindness—even with their opponent. One specific example occurred recently in my home. One of my boys wrestled a boy from another school and won the match. During the competition, my son was a lion seeking to physically dominate his opponent. After the match, my son spoke with the boy and started a friendship that extended to the next week when they were at a tournament. They did not wrestle again since they were in different weight classes, but they were rooting for each other and giving one another compliments after subsequent matches.

Every child is unique. Your son might not be at all interested in sports, but God still calls him to stand up for the truth and protect the weak. That's what it means to be a lion in our world. Physical strength is not the measure of a man. God's call is for men to use their strength to care for the weak and needy. So use your boy's interests and activities to help him think biblically about when and how to exercise his strength. Our boys need to learn to use their strength for God-ordained purposes. They also need to be full of grace, compassion, kindness, and sacrificial love for others. We need to teach them the wisdom to know when each is required.

Teach them to lead appropriately.

If you are a father of teenage boys, you know exactly what I am talking about. For those not quite there yet, now is the time to prepare. I believe that

God designed men to lead. They are leaders in their homes and they are leaders in their churches. As a father, I want my boys to learn how to lead. They have a responsibility before God, the church, and their families to take that leadership. However, boys often make several mistakes as they learn to lead.

1. Boys often mistake leading for dictating. This is an easy mistake to make. After all, being a leader means others are following—doing what you say. Perhaps your son has even seen you model this behavior. So it's easy for him to imagine that leadership means being in a place of honor and authority where he can bark out orders to everyone else. But dictatorship in the church and in the home does not honor God (Ephesians 6:4; 1 Peter 5) and it encourages rebellion. Boys need to learn that being a leader means adopting the mind-set of a servant. In Matthew 20 Jesus contrasts his type of leadership with usual leadership in the world. The first is characterized by service and concern for others. The latter is about telling people what to do. Thus, our boys will often try to lead people who are weaker than they are, taking advantage of their superior strength, size, intellect, verbal skills, social status, theological knowledge, or whatever gifts or abilities they may possess to impose their

will on others. They need to learn that leadership is serving others.

2. Boys learning to lead often try to lead the wrong people—commonly, their mother. I applaud and support the leadership efforts of boys. But boys often try to exercise that leadership with their mother. Boys are supposed to honor their father *and mother*. That means, among other things, that the mother retains her position of authority in the life of her son. Your son needs to know that when he is at home, he is not the leader. He is a follower, of both you and his mother. It is important at this stage that you, as father, make sure that your boys understand this point. This may require some frank conversations. In the end, however, this will be a tremendous blessing to your boys and their future families. It is important to train our sons both in appropriate leadership and appropriate submission because in reality they will be called to both at various times and in various roles in life.

3. Boys fail to take opportunities when they arise. While we need to help our boys understand that they are not leaders in the home, there are a lot of other opportunities for leadership around them. God calls us to teach our children to live out their faith

in all kinds of situations (Deuteronomy 6:6–7). So we, as their fathers, need to help them seize those opportunities. One such illustration presented itself recently. One of my boys was involved in leadership training at his school. At the end of the training the dads were invited to a lunch with the boys. As we were talking vaguely about leadership, I suggested that two of the boys take the last pizza box and walk around offering pizza to the other boys and their fathers. The boys obliged and took leadership in that situation. They ensured, through service, that every boy had enough to eat. Here was a time when leadership was not just a discussion, it was an activity. Look for ways to help your boys see and take opportunities for leadership. It is highly likely, if not certain, that your church and your school have many leadership gaps. If your son is reluctant to take leadership, ask him why. He may be afraid that he will not know what to do or that he will fail. This is a wonderful opportunity to teach perseverance and humility, both of which are necessary for effective leadership and which grow primarily through learning to handle failure. You may feel ill-equipped for such conversations because they reflect your own fears about leading, but this is a good opportunity for you to take a step of faith. Whatever your own feelings about leading, you and your son can depend on Christ to teach you both how to lead with his character.[3]

Teach them to be workers.

God has given us a responsibility to manage and care for his creation. It is one of the primary ways we bear his image in the world, and thus is a source of great blessing. Our boys are free to enjoy all sorts of blessings in life, but when they overindulge, those things can create "me monsters." They no longer see work as good and important, but as an impediment to their own personal pleasure. For this reason, it is good for our boys to be active and to restrict sources of entertainment (TV, video games, electronics) to manageable levels.

Personally, I think boys should be productively working as soon as possible. I greatly enjoyed watching one of my boys have his first summer job. It was the first time in his life that he had to be somewhere at 8 a.m. every day during the summer. There were days when he was sore, tired, and bored. But he learned to persevere. He learned that being a man involves working, and that working is not always doing exactly what you want to do when you want to do it. Many of his friends quit the job toward the end of the summer because "they wanted a break." Thankfully, my son did not. He worked to the end. In the process he learned at least two valuable lessons: (1) Men work. God designed us to work, and work is good for us. (2) When you work hard, other opportunities arise. The following summer, he was one of the first to be offered a job. That is a lesson you cannot learn in a classroom or on a living room couch while playing video games.

Conclusion

Fathers, remember that you do not have to accomplish all these things on your own. The Lord is at work in your life and in the lives of your boys. Weaknesses and mistakes are part of our continued struggle with sin, but thanks be to God that where sin abounds, grace abounds the more (Romans 5:20). Even if the task of raising boys seems overwhelming, you never do it alone. There is great hope because God is working both in and through you, and he promises to continue working until he perfects you at Christ's coming. So depend on him, trust him, and pray that the Lord would give you the grace, strength, and wisdom to raise your boys for his honor and glory.

Endnotes

1. I have the joy of being a parent to two boys and one girl. All are precious, and raising them is one of the great earthly joys that Stephanie and I have the privilege to experience.

2. We realize that some boys are molested by their father, stepfather, or other male role model. That is a travesty. There are many other minibooks in this series that address the matter of suffering. I am speaking about godly affection in this section.

3. Steve Viars, *Leadership: How to Guide Others with Integrity* (Greensboro, NC: New Growth Press, 2012).

Simple, Quick, Biblical

Advice on Complicated Counseling Issues
for Pastors, Counselors, and Individuals

MINIBOOK

CATEGORIES

- Personal Change
- Marriage & Parenting
- Medical & Psychiatric Issues
- Women's Issues
- Singles
- Military